I Can Read Music
A NOTE SPELLER FOR PIANO

By Nancy and Randall Faber

Contents

Special thanks and acknowledgment to
Crystal Bowman for the StoryRhymes.

ISBN 978-1-61677-227-7

Copyright © 1999 Dovetree Productions, Inc. (ASCAP).
c/o FABER PIANO ADVENTURES, 3042 Creek Dr., Ann Arbor, MI 48108
International Copyright Secured.   All Rights Reserved.   Printed in U.S.A.
WARNING: The music, text, *StoryRhymes,* design, and graphics in this publication are protected by copyright law.
Any duplication is an infringement of U.S. copyright law.

Teacher Note: The four pages of Lesson 1 review important reading concepts covered in *I Can Read Music*, Books 1 and 2.

Guide Note Review

Study the color illustration to review the seven "guide notes" on the Grand Staff.

The first letter of each word gives the note name.

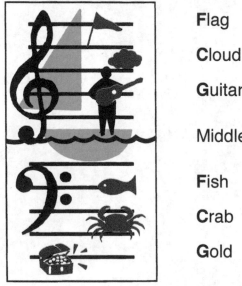

Flag

Cloud

Guitar

Middle C

Fish

Crab

Gold

Write the seven guide notes on the Grand Staff below. (Use whole notes.)

Name the notes in the boxes.

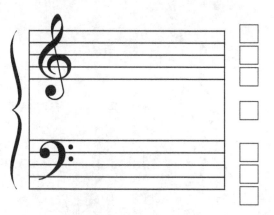

Now play and name aloud the seven guide notes on the keyboard.

First play going *up* the staff, then coming *down* the staff.

Write the letter names for the guide notes below.

Extra Credit: Play the above examples on the piano for *5 extra points each.*
Hint: Watch for changes of hand position.

Perfect Score: 30

With extra credit: 60

Your Score: _____

The Play
(Review of the Seven Guide Notes)
Words by Crystal Bowman

This *StoryRhyme* reviews the seven guide notes you have learned. (See page 2.)

Draw a **guide note** on the staff for each **circled letter** in the word.
(Remember to use one of the seven guide notes.) Enjoy reading the *StoryRhyme*!

Ex.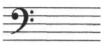

I have a ⓕeature role in the Middle SⒸhool play.

I've praⒸtiⒸed and I've memorized the words I'm ⓖoing to say.

I have the most important part; I've ⓖot to ⓖet it right.

Perhaps I'll be a ⓕamous star on Ⓒenter stage tonight.

I'm just a little nervous. In ⓕaⒸt, I'm really sⒸared!

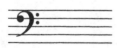

That's why I've praⒸtiⒸed and rehearsed; I need to be prepared.
I think I'll practice one more time,

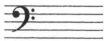

Let's see, it ⓖoes like this: "Thanks for Ⓒominⓖ here tonight.
　　　　　　　　　　　　　　　Now you are dismissed."

(Your teacher may ask you to play the guide notes in the *StoryRhyme* on the piano.)

Interval Review
(2nd, 3rd, 4th, 5th, 6th)

Interval Tower

First study the Interval Tower. Then draw a line from each example to the correct floor (interval) of the tower.

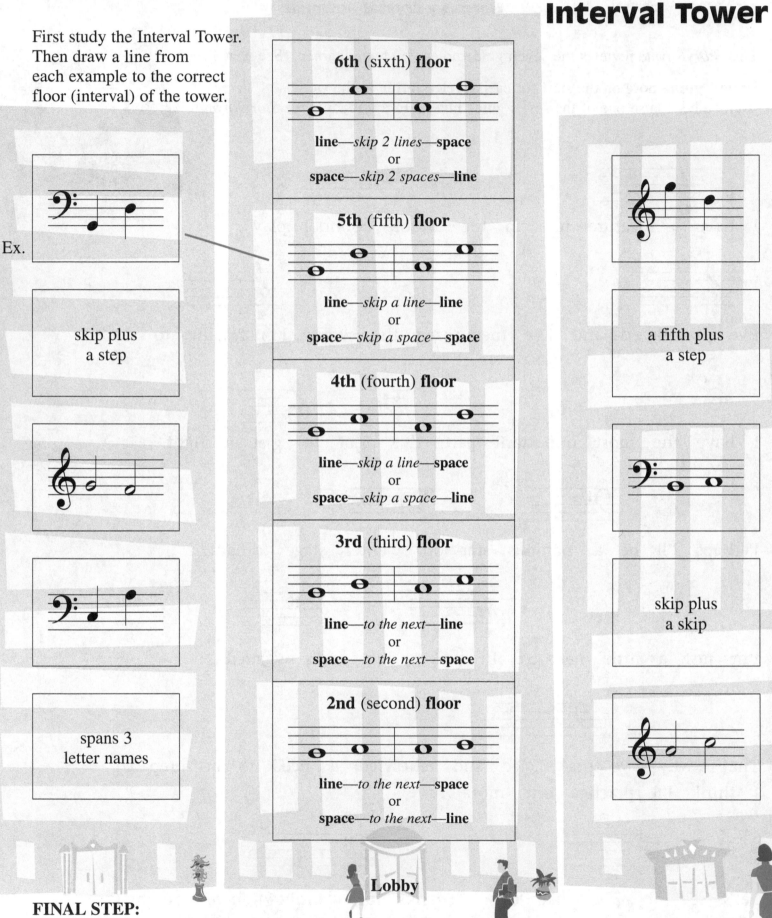

6th (sixth) **floor**

line—*skip 2 lines*—**space**
or
space—*skip 2 spaces*—**line**

5th (fifth) **floor**

line—*skip a line*—**line**
or
space—*skip a space*—**space**

4th (fourth) **floor**

line—*skip a line*—**space**
or
space—*skip a space*—**line**

3rd (third) **floor**

line—*to the next*—**line**
or
space—*to the next*—**space**

2nd (second) **floor**

line—*to the next*—**space**
or
space—*to the next*—**line**

Ex.

skip plus a step

spans 3 letter names

a fifth plus a step

skip plus a skip

Lobby

FINAL STEP:
Your teacher will choose an interval (2nd, 3rd, 4th, 5th, 6th). Describe how you can recognize that interval on the staff.

4

Review of Sharps, Flats, and Naturals

A *sharp* **raises** the pitch (tone) a half step.

Play the key one half step higher.

A *flat* **lowers** the pitch (tone) a half step.

Play the key one half step lower.

A *natural* **cancels** a sharp or flat.

A *natural* is always a white key.

These exercises review the *guide notes* with **sharps**, **flats**, and **naturals**. Name the notes in the blanks. Then play them on the piano.

Crawling Up with Sharps

1.

Note names: __G__ __G#__ ___ ___ ___ ___ ___ ___ ___ ___ ___ ___

Crawling Down with Flats

2.

___ ___ ___ ___ ___ ___ ___ ___ ___ ___

Sightread this exercise without writing note names.

Crawling "Naturally"

3.

Lesson 2

Upper and Lower Neighbor Tones

(More about 2nds)

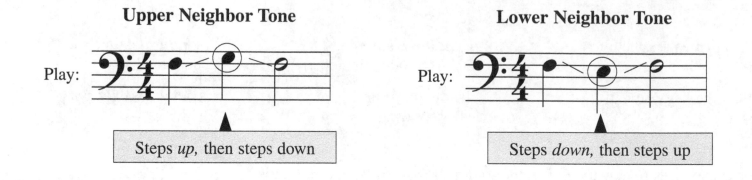

Upper Neighbor Tone

Play:

Steps *up*, then steps down

Lower Neighbor Tone

Play:

Steps *down*, then steps up

Circle *upper neighbor* or *lower neighbor* for each musical example.
Then name the notes in the blanks given.

Extra Credit: Play the above examples using the fingerings given. (1 point per note)
Notice each example begins with a guide note.

Perfect Score: 30

With extra credit: 60

Your Score: _____

FF1227

Sightreading Bonanza!

Each sightreading melody below begins on a guide note.

Your teacher will ask you to sightread this page and will keep a record of your progress with "Home Runs" and "Foul Balls."

Home Run = correct note   **Foul Ball = incorrect note or rhythm**

Teacher Note: Record the number of incorrect notes and rhythms under "Foul Balls." For "Home Runs," subtract the number of "Foul Balls" from the Perfect Score (80) given at the bottom of the page.

Sightreading Tips: 1. Set a steady beat by counting one "free" measure.
2. Keep your eyes on the music.
3. Play rather slowly, always moving your eyes ahead.
4. Keep going no matter what!

Perfect Score: 80

Date:

FF1227

Lesson 3   Grand Staff Tour with 3rds

(For a review of 3rds, see page 4.)

Thinking in 3rds

The LINE notes move up and down the grand staff in 3rds.

1. First shade the *five guide notes* that are written on lines.

2. Then name each line note in the blank given. Think 3rds (skips)!

3. Play each line note on the keyboard, saying its name aloud.
   Play from *lowest* to *highest*, then *highest* to *lowest*.

Ex. **G** ___ ___ ___ ___ ___ ___

The SPACE notes also move up and down the grand staff in 3rds.

1. First shade the *two guide notes* that are written on spaces.

2. Then name each space note in the blank given. Think 3rds (skips)!

3. Play each space note on the keyboard, saying its name aloud.
   Play from *lowest* to *highest*, then *highest* to *lowest*.

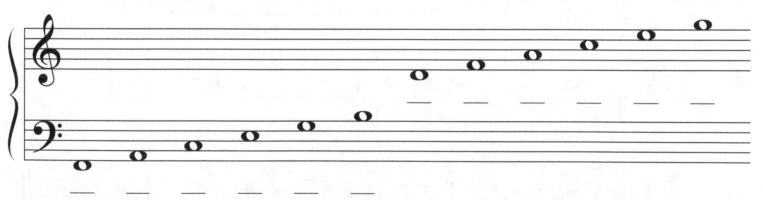

Two Reading Challenges: (For your daily practice this week)

1. Name the LINE NOTES of the grand staff from bottom to top (Low G to High F).
   Do not look at this page! Your teacher will time you.   **Your fastest time:** _____

2. Name the SPACE NOTES of the grand staff from bottom to top (Low F to High G).
   Do not look at this page! Your teacher will time you.   **Your fastest time:** _____

FF1227

My Room

Words by Crystal Bowman

Draw the note that is a **3rd up** or **down** from the note given.
Name both notes in the blanks and enjoy reading the *StoryRhyme*!

I hate to __ l __ an my __ e __ room, but my mother says I must. She doesn't like

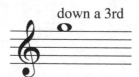

the messy floor, the fin __ __ rprints, or dust. I think it's quite __ ttra __ tiv __ ,

with an interesting decor. I've piled all my dirty __ loth __ s so neatly on the floor.

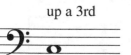

My so __ c __ r ball and baseball are much easier to __ in __

sitting on my windowsill, beneath the mini- __ lin __ s.   The __ __ ndy wrappers
on my desk are really not that old.

The pop __ __ ns on my bookshelf look __ r __ at with all that mold.

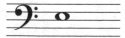

I like coll __ __ ting magazines; I need one hundred more. It only takes a day or two

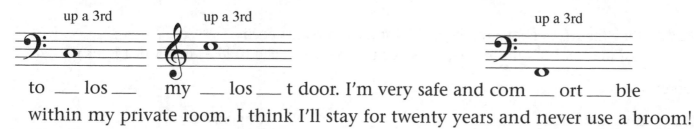

to __ los __ my __ los __ t door. I'm very safe and com __ ort __ ble
within my private room. I think I'll stay for twenty years and never use a broom!

(Your teacher may ask you to play the 3rds in the *StoryRhyme* on the piano.)

Triads: Thinking with 3rds

A triad is a 3-note chord built with 3rds.

C triad

Example:

G
E — 3rd
C — 3rd

"Spell" the triads below by naming the notes from bottom to top (lowest to highest).
Think 3rds!

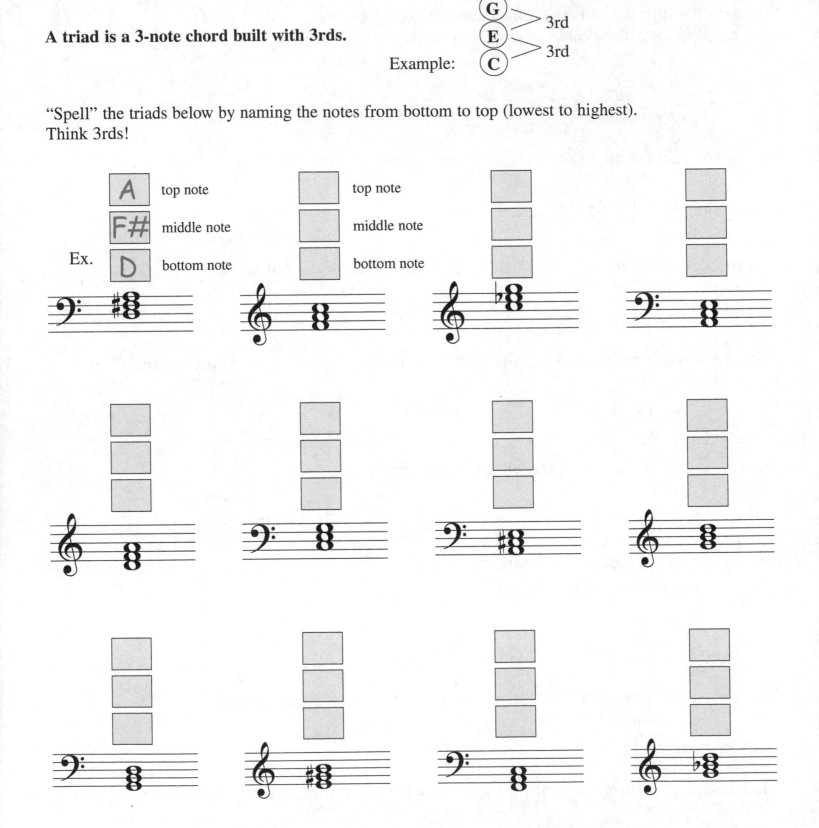

Extra Credit: Play the triads above on the piano for 2 extra points each.
(At the teacher's discretion, the student may name each triad as major or minor.)

Perfect Score: 36

With extra credit: 60

Your Score: _____

FF1227

Sightreading Bonanza!

Sightread these musical examples that use **triads**.
Be alert for *blocked* triads (notes played together) and *broken* triads (notes played separately).

Remember to set a slow, steady beat with one "free" measure before you begin.

Your teacher will keep a record of your progress with "Beautiful Notes" (correct notes) and "Bonker Notes" (incorrect notes).

Do this page with your teacher each week and write down your score.

Perfect Score: 65

Date:

_____ (1st Week)	_____ Beautiful Notes	_____ Bonker Notes
_____ (2nd Week)	_____ Beautiful Notes	_____ Bonker Notes
_____ (3rd Week)	_____ Beautiful Notes	_____ Bonker Notes

Passing Tones

The notes of a triad are called **chord tones**.

C triad

Play: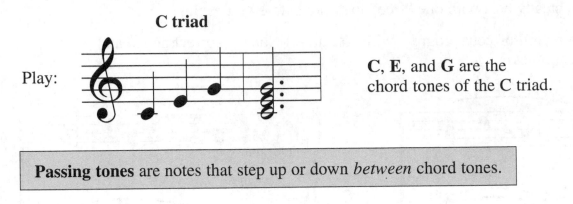

C, **E**, and **G** are the
chord tones of the C triad.

Passing tones are notes that step up or down *between* chord tones.

Play this example that uses **passing tones** between the notes of a C chord.

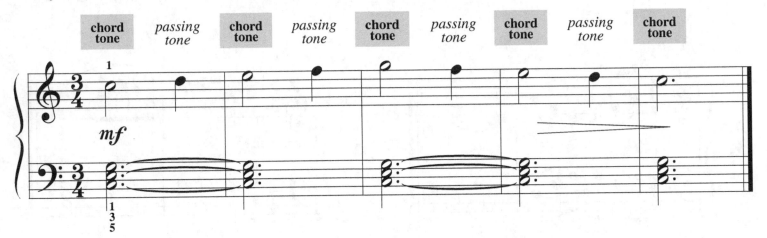

Circle the **passing tones** between the chord tones of the C triad. (Hint: There are 4.) Then play.

Circle the **passing tones** between the chord tones of the G triad. (Hint: There are 8.) Then play.

Sightreading Bonanza!

Upper Neighbors, Lower Neighbors, and Passing Tones

(For review of upper and lower neighbor tones, see page 6.)

For each musical example, write: **U.N.** for Upper Neighbor tone
or
L.N. for Lower Neighbor tone
or
P.T. for Passing tone

Then sightread each example. Your teacher will keep a record of your progress with "Cool Notes" (correct notes) and "Crazy Notes" (incorrect notes).

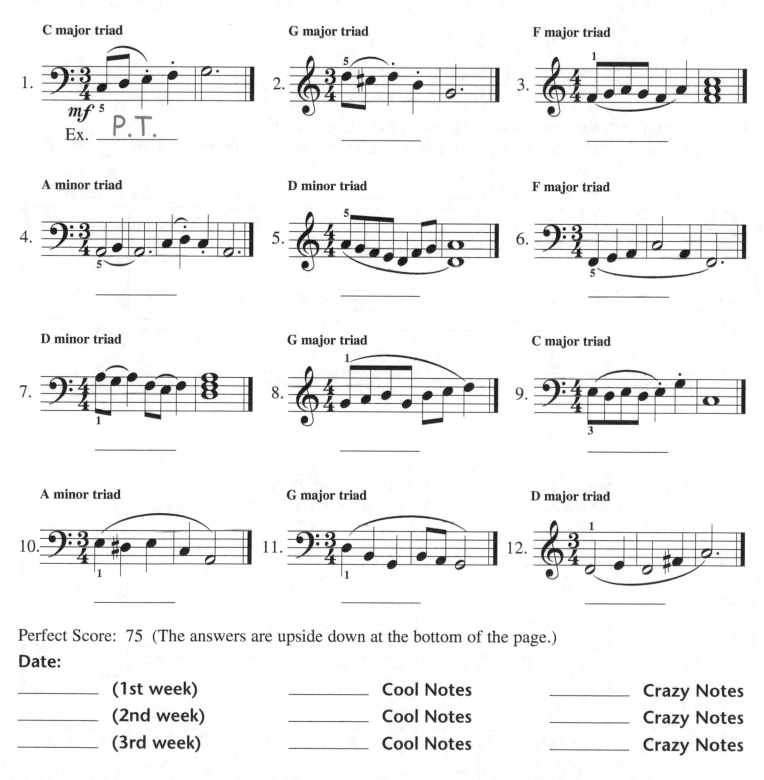

Perfect Score: 75 (The answers are upside down at the bottom of the page.)

Date:

_____ (1st week)　　_____ Cool Notes　　_____ Crazy Notes

_____ (2nd week)　　_____ Cool Notes　　_____ Crazy Notes

_____ (3rd week)　　_____ Cool Notes　　_____ Crazy Notes

Answers: 1. P.T. 2. L.N. 3. P.T. 4. U.N. 5. P.T. 6. P.T. 7. L.N. 8. P.T. 9. P.T. 10. L.N. 11. P.T. 12. U.N.

4ths and 5ths
on the Grand Staff

(For review of 4ths and 5ths, see page 4.)

Remember when writing a 4th or 5th, count each
line and space including the *first* and *last* notes.

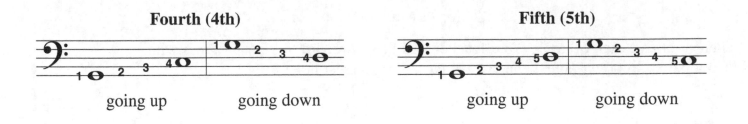

Fourth (4th)

going up   going down

Fifth (5th)

going up   going down

Draw a **4th up** or **down** from these guide notes. (Use whole notes.)
Name the notes in the blanks. Then play the 4ths on the piano using the fingering given.

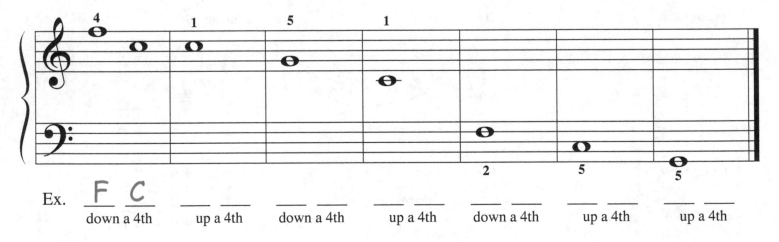

Ex.   F C   ___ ___   ___ ___   ___ ___   ___ ___   ___ ___   ___ ___
      down a 4th   up a 4th   down a 4th   up a 4th   down a 4th   up a 4th   up a 4th

Draw a **5th up** or **down** from each of these guide notes. (Use whole notes.)
Name the notes in the blanks. Then play the 5ths on the piano using the fingerings given.

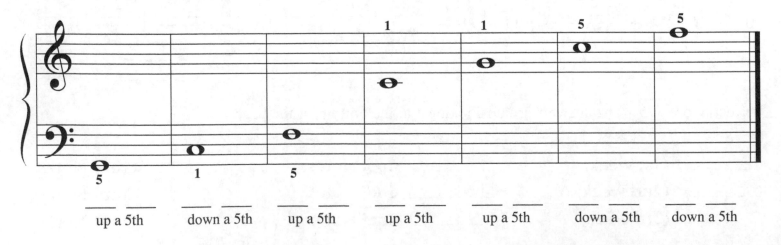

___ ___   ___ ___   ___ ___   ___ ___   ___ ___   ___ ___   ___ ___
up a 5th   down a 5th   up a 5th   up a 5th   up a 5th   down a 5th   down a 5th

FF1227

Tuna Sandwich

Words by Crystal Bowman

Draw the note that is a **2nd**, **3rd**, **4th**, or **5th up** or **down** from the note given.
Name both notes in the blanks and enjoy reading the *StoryRhyme*!

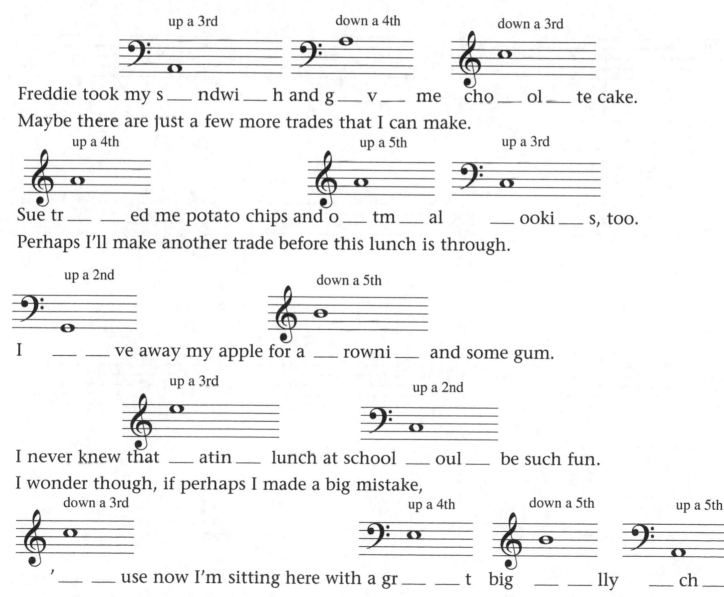

I got my ___ roth ___ r's s ___ n ___ wich in my lunchbox by mist ___ k ___ .
This one smells like tunafish; It's not the kind I take.

I cle ___ re ___ my throat politely; I rais ___ ___ my hand and s ___ i ___ ,
"Would anybody like to trade for tunafish on bread?"

Freddie took my s ___ ndwi ___ h and g ___ v ___ me   cho ___ ol ___ te cake.
Maybe there are just a few more trades that I can make.

Sue tr ___ ___ ed me potato chips and o ___ tm ___ al   ___ ooki ___ s, too.
Perhaps I'll make another trade before this lunch is through.

I   ___ ___ ve away my apple for a ___ rowni ___ and some gum.

I never knew that ___ atin ___ lunch at school ___ oul ___ be such fun.
I wonder though, if perhaps I made a big mistake,

'___ ___ use now I'm sitting here with a gr ___ ___ t big ___ lly ___ ch ___ !

(Your teacher may ask you to play the intervals in the *StoryRhyme* on the piano.)

Stemming Notes

Stems on notes can go up or down. Learn this rule for stemming notes correctly.

- For notes *on* or *above* line 3, the stem goes DOWN.

- For notes *below* line 3, the stem goes UP.

line 3

Stemming Practice

Draw stems correctly on the notes below.
Then write the **note names** in the blanks and the **interval name** in the box.

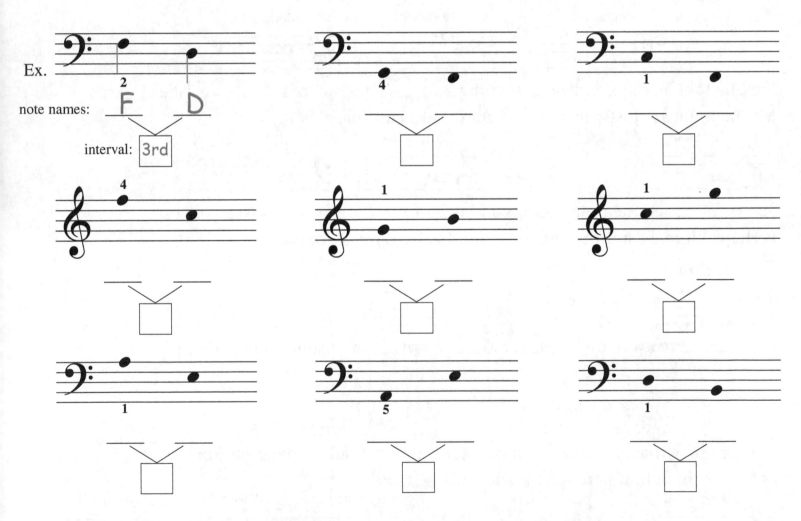

Ex.

note names: F   D

interval: 3rd

Extra Credit: Play the above examples on the piano for 2 extra points each.

Perfect Score: 27

With extra credit: 45   **Your Score:** _____

FF1227

Sightreading Bonanza!

Sightread these musical examples that use **2nds**, **3rds**, **4ths**, and **5ths**, as well as *sharps, flats,* and *naturals.* (For a review of sharps, flats, and naturals, see page 5.)

Your teacher will keep a record of your progress with "Delightful Notes" (correct notes) and "Dreadful Notes" (incorrect notes).

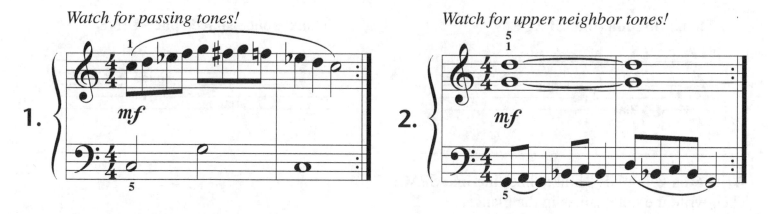

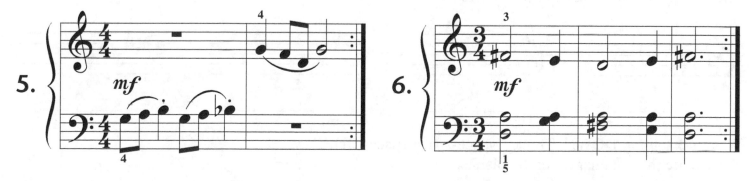

Perfect Score: 75

Date:

_____ (1st week)	_____ Delightful Notes	_____ Dreadful Notes
_____ (2nd week)	_____ Delightful Notes	_____ Dreadful Notes
_____ (3rd week)	_____ Delightful Notes	_____ Dreadful Notes

Writing 6ths

(For a review of 6ths, see page 4.)

A Shortcut for Writing 6ths

Rather than counting *each* line and space, you may prefer this shortcut for writing **6ths**.

Think: **line-line-line-SPACE**   Think: **space-space-space-LINE**

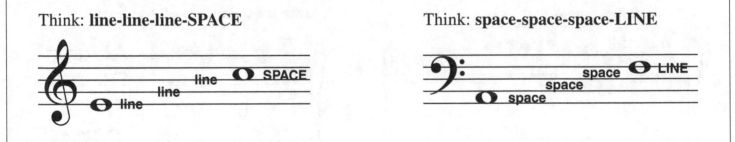

Write **6ths** going UP. Think: "line-line-line-SPACE."
Then write the note names in the blanks.

Ex. G   E   ___   ___ ___   ___ ___   ___ ___

Write **6ths** going DOWN. Think: "line-line-line-SPACE."
Then write the note names in the blanks.

___ ___   ___ ___   ___ ___   ___ ___

Write **6ths** going UP. Think: "space-space-space-LINE."
Then write the note names in the blanks.

___ ___   ___ ___   ___ ___   ___ ___

Write **6ths** going DOWN. Think: "space-space-space-LINE."
Then write the note names in the blanks.

___ ___   ___ ___   ___ ___   ___ ___

Extra Credit: Your teacher may ask you to play the 6ths you have written.

No Fair

Words by Crystal Bowman

Draw the note that is a **6th up** or **down** from the note given.
Name both notes in the blanks and enjoy reading the *StoryRhyme!*

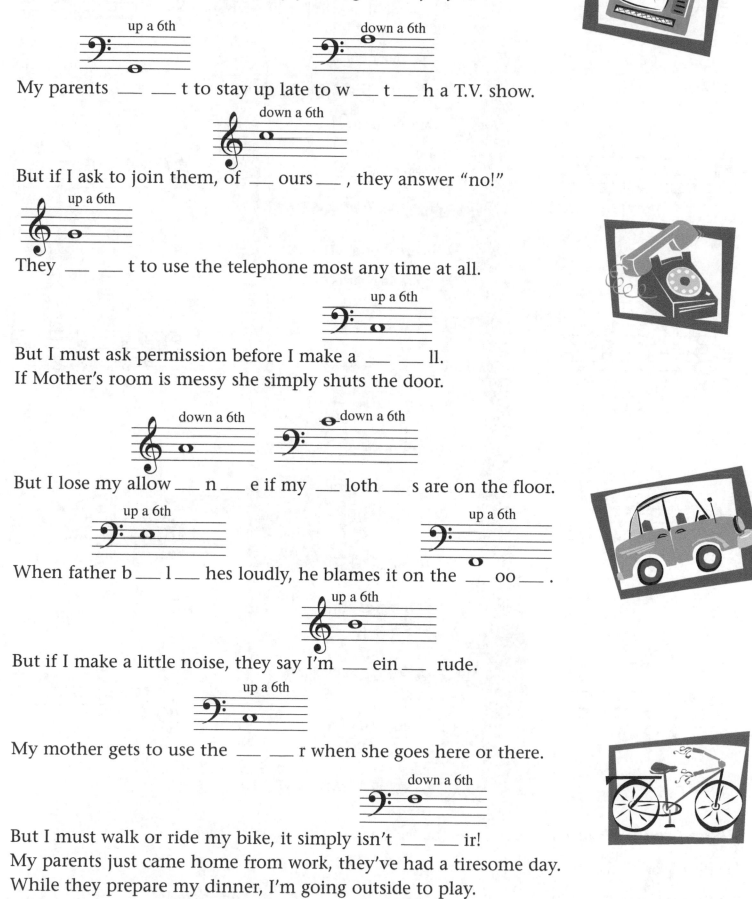

My parents ___ ___ t to stay up late to w ___ t ___ h a T.V. show.

But if I ask to join them, of ___ ours ___ , they answer "no!"

They ___ ___ t to use the telephone most any time at all.

But I must ask permission before I make a ___ ___ ll.
If Mother's room is messy she simply shuts the door.

But I lose my allow ___ n ___ e if my ___ loth ___ s are on the floor.

When father b ___ l ___ hes loudly, he blames it on the ___ oo ___ .

But if I make a little noise, they say I'm ___ ein ___ rude.

My mother gets to use the ___ ___ r when she goes here or there.

But I must walk or ride my bike, it simply isn't ___ ___ ir!
My parents just came home from work, they've had a tiresome day.
While they prepare my dinner, I'm going outside to play.

(Your teacher may ask you to play the 6ths in the *StoryRhyme* on the piano.)

Interval Matching Game

Draw a connecting line from each musical example to the matching interval box.

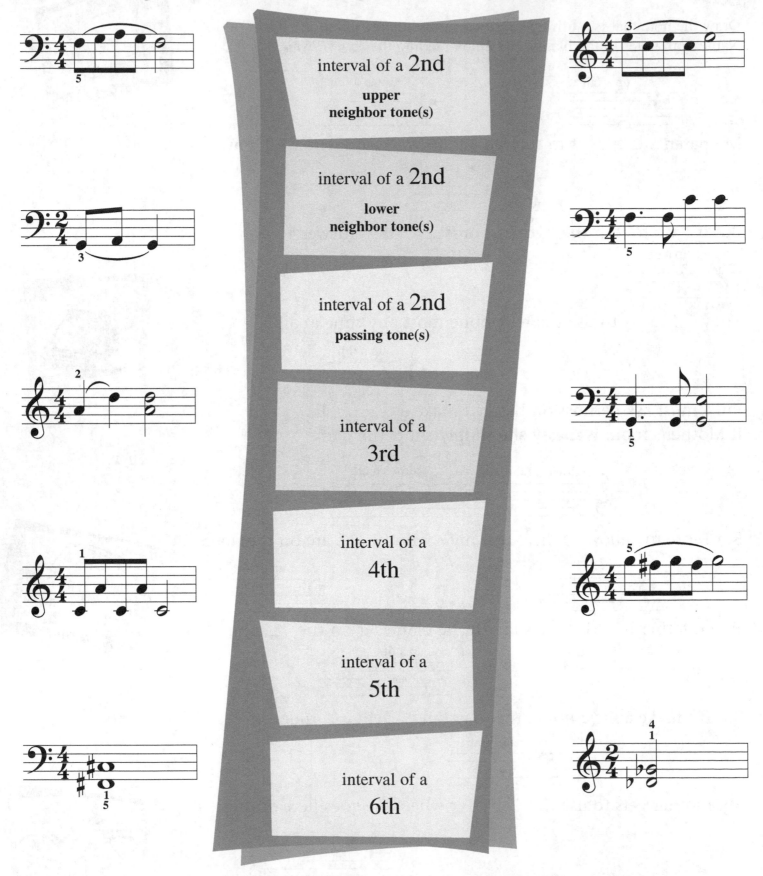

Extra Credit: Play the above examples on the piano for 5 extra points each.

Perfect Score: 50

With extra credit: 100

Your Score: _____

Sightreading Bonanza!

These musical examples use **2nds**, **3rds**, **4ths**, **5ths**, and **6ths**.
Practice sightreading these longer melodies. Play rather slowly.

Your teacher will keep a record of your progress with "Fun Notes"
(correct notes) and "Funky Notes" (incorrect notes).

Each week try for an improved sightreading score!

1.

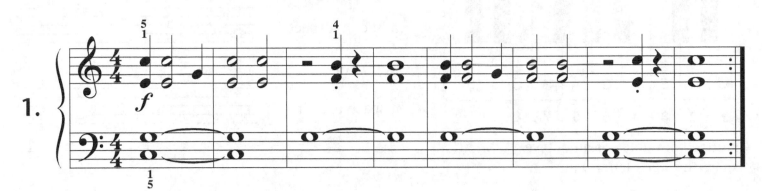

2.

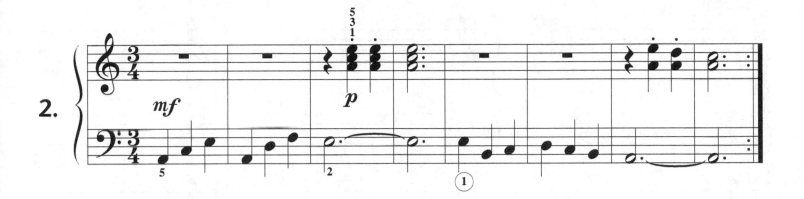

3.

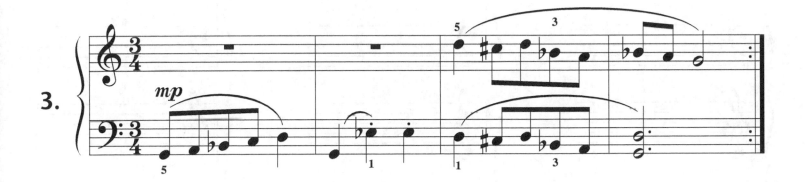

Perfect Score: 60

Date:

_____ (1st week)　　_____ Fun Notes　　_____ Funky Notes

_____ (2nd week)　　_____ Fun Notes　　_____ Funky Notes

_____ (3rd week)　　_____ Fun Notes　　_____ Funky Notes

The Octave

"Oct-" means 8. (As in <u>oct</u>opus—8 legs; <u>oct</u>agon—8 sides)

The interval of an **octave** spans 8 letter names. (8ve is the abbreviation for octave.)

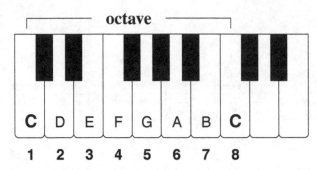

An **octave** is:

a line to a space

or

a space to a line

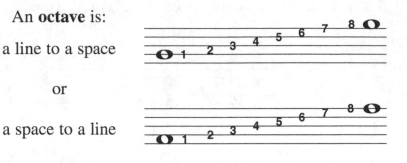

Notice both notes of an octave share the *same* letter name.

Write an **octave above** and **below** the note given on the grand staff.

Example:

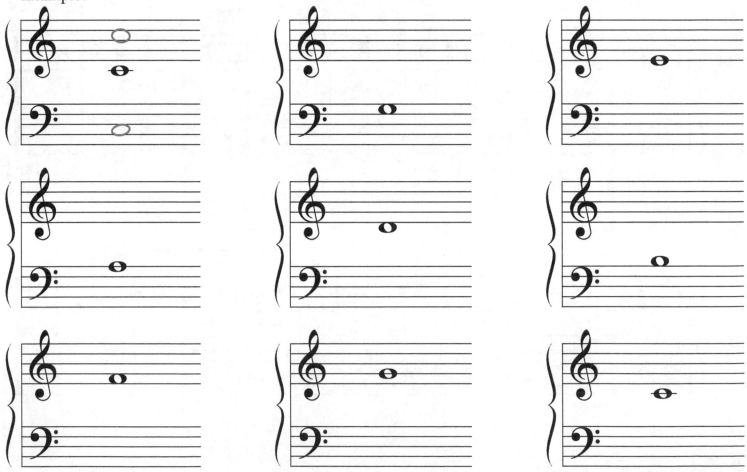

Extra Credit: Play the octaves above on the keyboard for 3 extra points each.

Perfect Score: 18

With extra credit: 45

Your Score: _____

Interval Sleuth

Put a ✔ in the box for the correct interval names.
Give yourself 5 points for each correct answer.

octave – 5th ☐
or
octave – 4th ☐

4th – octave ☐
or
5th – octave ☐

6th – octave ☐
or
octave – 6th ☐

6th – 4th ☐
or
6th – 3rd ☐

3rd – octave ☐
or
3rd – 6th ☐

octave – 4th ☐
or
octave – 2nd ☐

6th – 3rd ☐
or
octave – 3rd ☐

3rd – 2nd ☐
or
3rd – 3rd ☐

4th – 5th ☐
or
5th – 4th ☐

6th – 5th ☐
or
6th – octave ☐

Extra Credit: Play the above examples on the piano for 5 extra points each.

Perfect Score: 50

With extra credit: 100   **Your Score:** _____

The 7th (Seventh)

The interval of a **7th** spans 7 letter names.

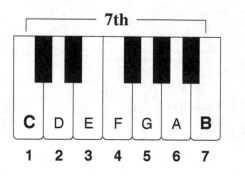

7th

C D E F G A B
1 2 3 4 5 6 7

A **7th** is:

a line to a line

or

a space to a space

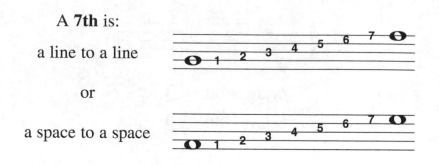

A Shortcut for Writing 7ths

Rather than counting *each* line and space, you may prefer this shortcut for writing 7ths.

Think: **an octave minus a 2nd (step)**

Write a **7th up** or **down** from the note given.
Then write the note names in the blanks.

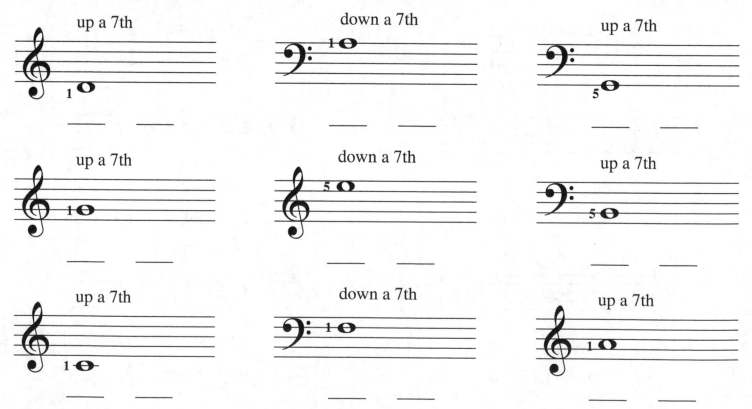

up a 7th

down a 7th

up a 7th

up a 7th

down a 7th

up a 7th

up a 7th

down a 7th

up a 7th

Extra Credit: Play the 7ths above on the keyboard for 2 extra points each.

Perfect Score: 27

With extra credit: 45

Your Score: _____

Chocolate Medicine

Words by Crystal Bowman

Draw the note that is a **7th up** or **down** from the note given.
Name both notes in the blanks and enjoy reading the *StoryRhyme*!

Chocolate flavor __ __   me __ i __ ine would taste so very good!

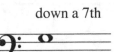

I know I'd __ l __ dly take it if my doctor said I should.

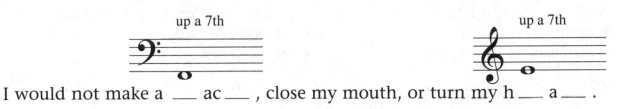

I would not make a __ ac __ , close my mouth, or turn my h __ a __ .

I would not make a fuss, or go and hi __ __   __ ene __ th

my b __ __ . If I had chocolate medicine, I know I'd love the taste.
I'd finish every single drop, it would not go to waste.

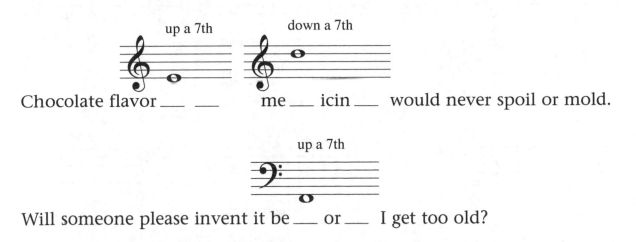

Chocolate flavor __ __   me __ icin __ would never spoil or mold.

Will someone please invent it be __ or __ I get too old?

(Your teacher may ask you to play the 7ths in the *StoryRhyme* on the piano.)

Cousins on the Staff
(Comparing 3rds, 5ths, and 7ths)

Think of 3rds, 5ths, and 7ths as "cousins."

How are **3rds**, **5ths**, and **7ths** alike?

Each of these intervals is a **line-to-a-line** or a **space-to-a-space**.

Play: **3rd** **5th** **7th**   Play: **3rd** **5th** **7th**

How are **3rds**, **5ths**, and **7ths** different?

- 3rds move line to the *next* line
- 5ths skip *one* line
- 7ths skip *two* lines

- 3rds move space to the *next* space
- 5ths skip *one* space
- 7ths skip *two* spaces

3rd **5th** **7th**   **3rd** **5th** **7th**

Writing 3rds, 5ths, and 7ths

Name the **interval** and then the **note names** for each example.
Then play the intervals on the piano.

Interval:

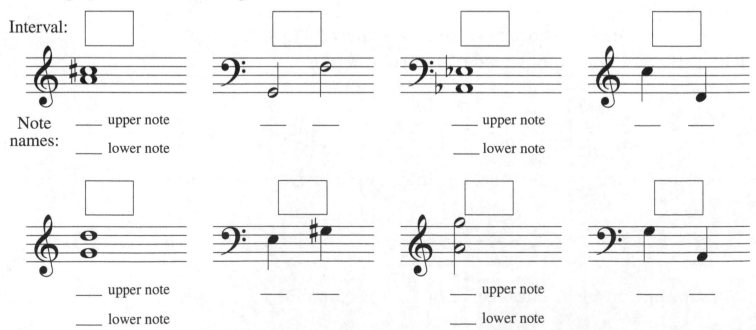

Note
names: ___ upper note   ___ ___   ___ upper note   ___ ___

___ lower note   ___ lower note

___ upper note   ___ ___   ___ upper note   ___ ___

___ lower note   ___ lower note

Sightreading Bonanza!

Sightread these musical examples that use all the intervals you have learned:

2nd, 3rd, 4th, 5th, 6th, 7th, and **octave**

Remember to set a slow, steady beat of one full measure before you begin.
Always keep your eyes moving ahead!

Your teacher will keep a record of your progress with "Delicious Notes"
(correct notes) and "Dangerous Notes" (incorrect notes).

Perfect Score: 75

Date:

_____	(1st week)	_____ Delicious Notes	_____ Dangerous Notes
_____	(2nd week)	_____ Delicious Notes	_____ Dangerous Notes
_____	(3rd week)	_____ Delicious Notes	_____ Dangerous Notes

Upper Ledger Lines

Short lines called *ledger lines* are used to write notes above the High G on the treble staff.

Find and play these **upper ledger notes** on the keyboard.
Say the letter names aloud.

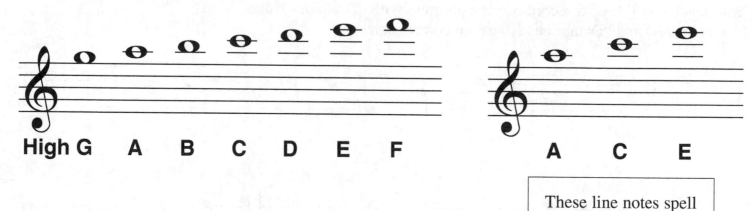

High G A B C D E F | **A C E**

> These line notes spell
> the word "ACE."

Spelling Bee

Spell the words given below using **only upper ledger notes**.
Hint: Cover the top of the page to challenge yourself.

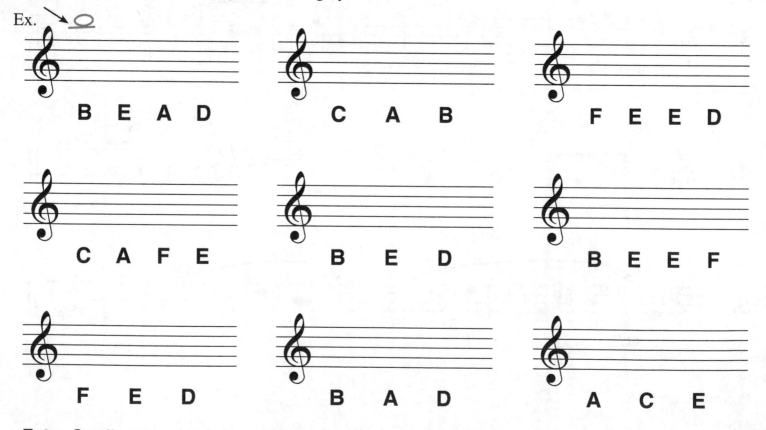

Ex.

B E A D   C A B   F E E D

C A F E   B E D   B E E F

F E D   B A D   A C E

Extra Credit: Play each ledger note "word" on the piano to hear how the melody sounds. (5 pts. each)

Perfect Score: 30

With extra credit: 75

Your Score: _____

Take It Up an Octave!

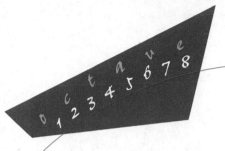

Name each note for the melody on the left.

Then write the *same* melody **one octave higher** on the staff to the right.
(The first example has been done for you.)

Ex.

A B C B A

Extra Credit: Play the melodies above for 50 extra points. (5 points each)

Perfect Score: 50

With extra credit: 100

Your Score: _____

Sightreading Bonanza!

Sightread these melodies that use **upper ledger notes**.
You may recognize some of the melodies.

First scan the music. Notice the *shape* of the melody (the
upward, downward, and repeated movement of the notes).

Your teacher will keep a record of your progress with "In-Tune Notes"
(correct notes) and "Out-of-Tune Notes" (incorrect notes).

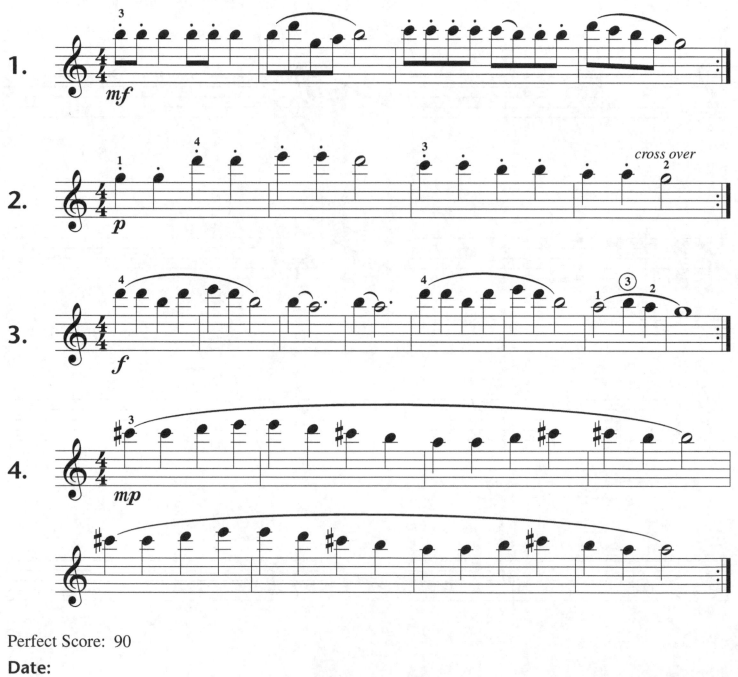

Perfect Score: 90

Date:

_____	(1st week)	_____	In-Tune Notes	_____ Out-of-Tune Notes
_____	(2nd week)	_____	In-Tune Notes	_____ Out-of-Tune Notes
_____	(3rd week)	_____	In-Tune Notes	_____ Out-of-Tune Notes

Lower Ledger Lines

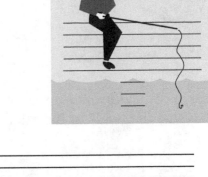

Ledger lines are also used to write notes *below* the Low F on the bass staff.

Find and play these **lower ledger notes** on the keyboard.
Say the letter names aloud.

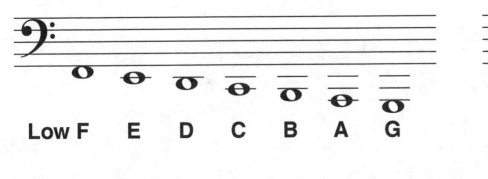

Low F   E   D   C   B   A   G

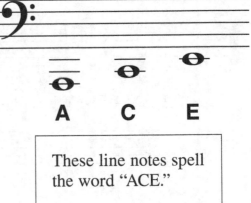

A   C   E

These line notes spell the word "ACE."

Interval Travel

Complete the intervals below by writing **lower ledger notes**.
Then name both notes in the blanks.
Hint: Cover the top of the page to challenge yourself.

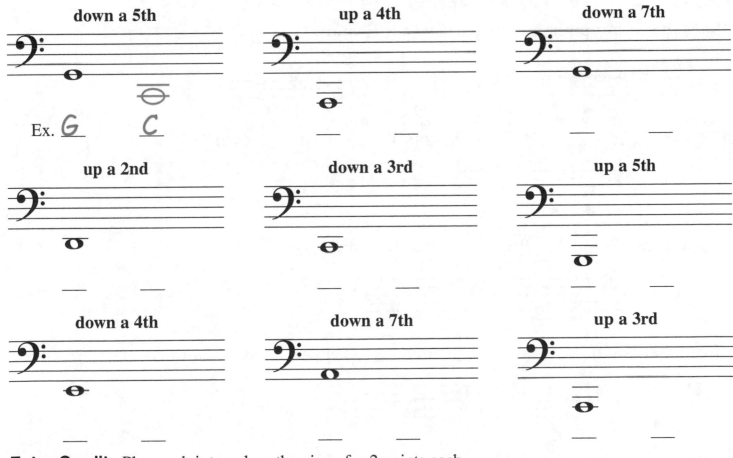

down a 5th

Ex. G   C

up a 4th

___   ___

down a 7th

___   ___

up a 2nd

___   ___

down a 3rd

___   ___

up a 5th

___   ___

down a 4th

___   ___

down a 7th

___   ___

up a 3rd

___   ___

Extra Credit: Play each interval on the piano for 2 points each.

Perfect Score: 27

With extra credit: 45

Your Score: _____

Pizza Time

Words by Crystal Bowman

This *StoryRhyme* uses only **lower ledger notes**.
Name the notes in the blanks and enjoy reading the *StoryRhyme*!

P __ pp __ roni, s __ u __ __ , and __ h __ s __ ! May I

have some pizz __ , please? __ h __ wy crusts are

extra ni __ __ . May I have another sli __ __ ?
Who's that other pizza for? May I have a little more?

Six more pi __ __ __ s then I'll stop. W __ sh it __ own

with soda pop. F__ __ lin __ just a little stuff __ __ ,

I think that I've h __ __ __ nou __ h. Pepperoni, sauce, and cheese;

No mor __ pizz __ for me, pl __ __ s __ !

(Your teacher may ask you to play the lower ledger notes in the *StoryRhyme* on the piano.)

Sightreading Bonanza!

Sightread these melodies that use **lower ledger notes**.
You may recognize some of the melodies.

First scan the music. Be alert for *sharps* and *ties*.

Your teacher will keep a record of your progress with "Marvelous Notes"
(correct notes) and "Monster Notes" (incorrect notes).

1.

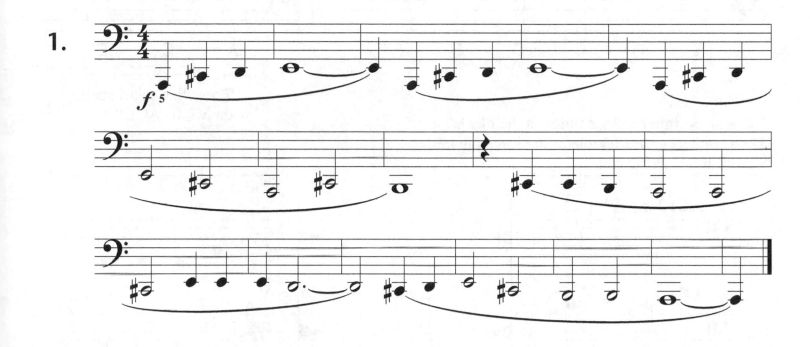

Notice the cross-over before you begin.

2.

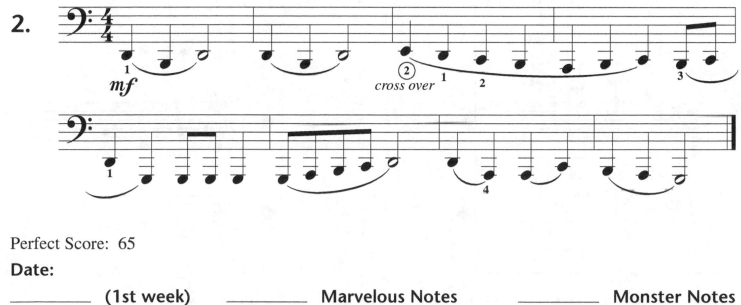

Perfect Score: 65

Date:

_____ (1st week)   _____ Marvelous Notes   _____ Monster Notes

_____ (2nd week)   _____ Marvelous Notes   _____ Monster Notes

_____ (3rd week)   _____ Marvelous Notes   _____ Monster Notes

Inner Ledger Lines
(for Left Hand)

Middle C is a ledger line note. When the L.H. plays notes *above* Middle C, **inner ledger lines** are used for the bass staff.

Find and play these inner ledger notes on the keyboard. Say the letter names aloud.

(A   B)   C   D   E   F

A   C   E

These line notes spell the word "ACE."

Name these **inner ledger notes** in the blanks. Then connect each example to the *same* pitches written in the treble clef.

Extra Credit: Play these L.H. inner ledger notes on the piano for 4 points each.

Perfect Score: 25

With extra credit: 45

Your Score: _____

Inner Ledger Lines
(for Right Hand)

When the R.H. plays notes *below* Middle C,
inner ledger lines are used for the treble staff.

Find and play these inner ledger notes on the keyboard. Say the letter names aloud.

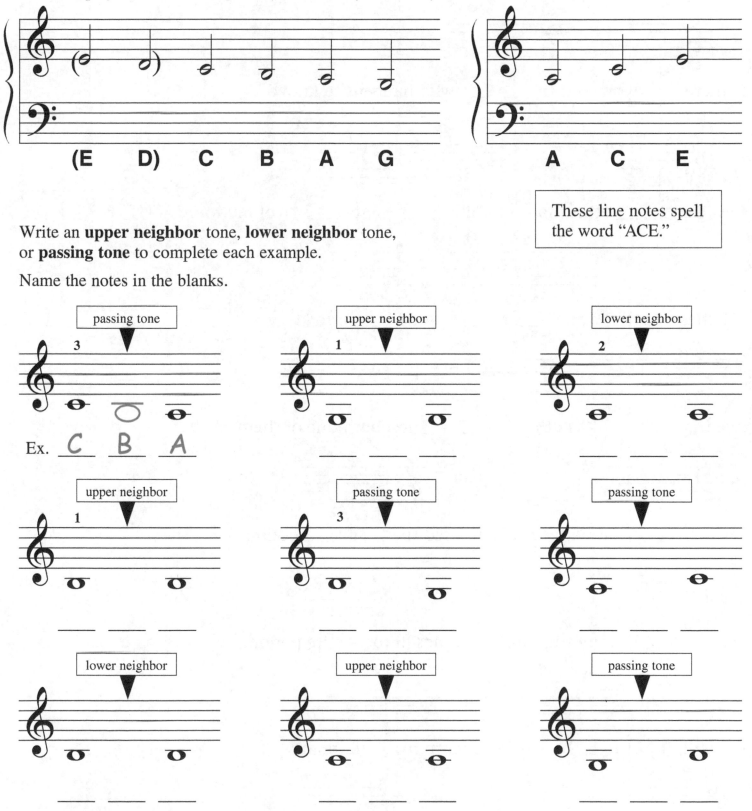

(E   D)   C   B   A   G   A   C   E

These line notes spell the word "ACE."

Write an **upper neighbor** tone, **lower neighbor** tone,
or **passing tone** to complete each example.

Name the notes in the blanks.

Extra Credit: Play these R.H. inner ledger notes on the piano for 1 point each.

Perfect Score: 36

With extra credit: 45   **Your Score:** _____

Mosquito Bite

Words by Crystal Bowman

This *StoryRhyme* uses **inner ledger notes** for the treble and bass clef.
Name the notes in the blanks and enjoy reading the *StoryRhyme*!

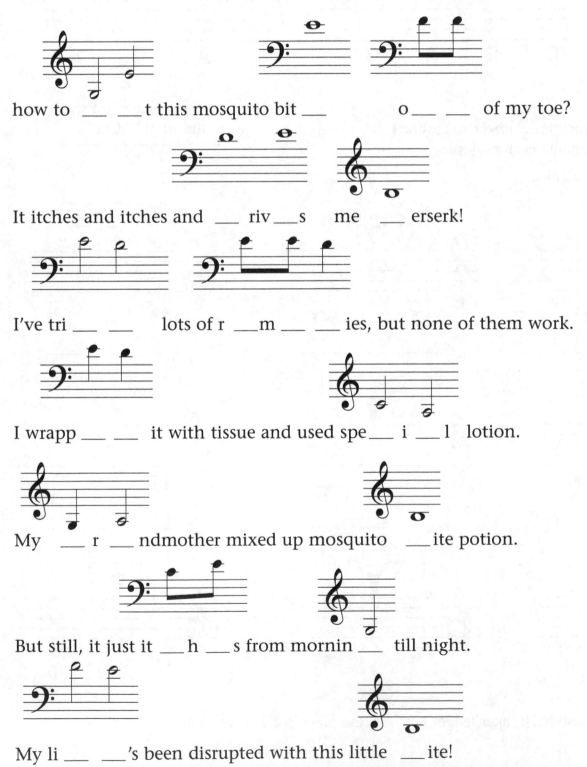

Is there ___ nyone out th ___ r ___ who happens to know

how to ___ ___ t this mosquito bit ___   o ___ ___ of my toe?

It itches and itches and ___ riv ___ s   me ___ erserk!

I've tri ___ ___   lots of r ___ m ___ ___ ies, but none of them work.

I wrapp ___ ___ it with tissue and used spe ___ i ___ l lotion.

My   ___ r ___ ndmother mixed up mosquito ___ ite potion.

But still, it just it ___ h ___ s from mornin ___ till night.

My li ___ ___'s been disrupted with this little ___ ite!

(Your teacher may ask you to play the inner ledger notes in the *StoryRhyme* on the piano.)

Sightreading Bonanza!

Sightread these melodies that use **inner ledger notes**.
You may recognize some of the melodies.

Your teacher will keep a record of your progress with "Lucky Notes"
(correct notes) and "Lopsided Notes" (incorrect notes).

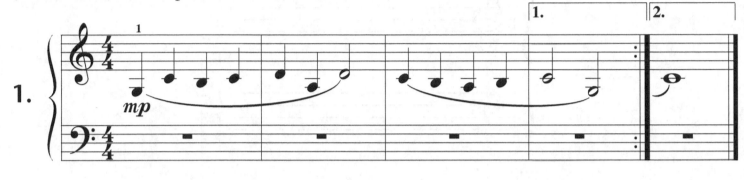

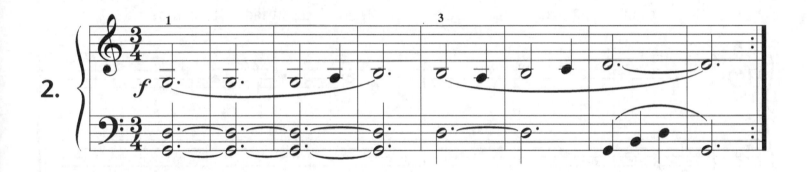

Notice the fingering changes before you begin.

Perfect Score: 60

Date:

_____ (1st week)	_____ Lucky Notes	_____ Lopsided Notes
_____ (2nd week)	_____ Lucky Notes	_____ Lopsided Notes
_____ (3rd week)	_____ Lucky Notes	_____ Lopsided Notes

1. Write the **seven guide notes** on the grand staff below. (Use whole notes.)
   Name the notes in the boxes. Then play each guide note on the piano.

2. Name the notes. Then identify the **triads** used in each measure.
   Play the broken triads on the keyboard.

___ triad   ___ triad   ___ triad   ___ triad   ___ triad   ___ triad   ___ triad

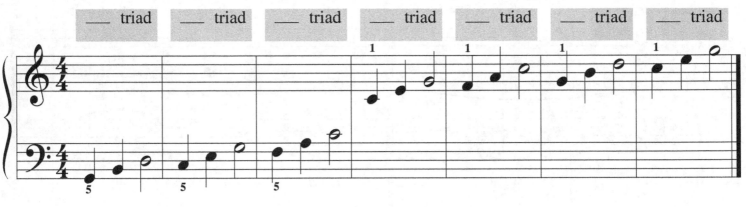

3. Name the **notes** in the blanks. Then name each **interval** in the box.
   Play the intervals on the keyboard. Use your own fingering.

FF12

4. Write **U.N.** (Upper Neighbor), **L.N.** (Lower Neighbor) or **P.T.** (Passing Tone)
for each measure below. Then sightread the melody at a moderately slow tempo.

5. Stem these notes correctly. Then play each on the piano.

6. Name three intervals that are always *line-to-line* or *space-to-space.*

___ , ___ , and ___

7. Name four intervals that are always *line-to-space* or *space-to-line.*

___ , ___ , ___ , and ___

8. Name these **upper ledger notes**. Play each on the piano.

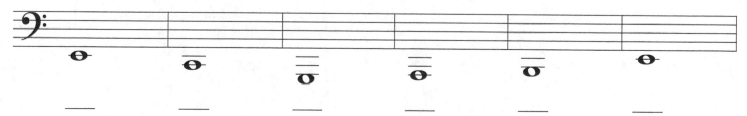

9. Name these **lower ledger notes**. Play each on the piano.

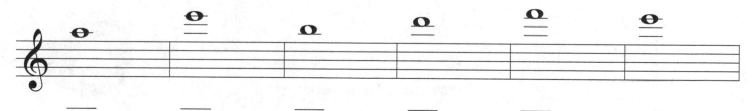

10. Name each note in the blank. Then write the *same* pitch using an **inner ledger note**.
Play each on the piano.

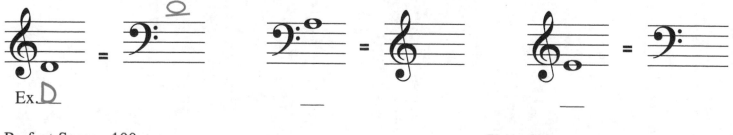

Ex. D

Perfect Score: 100

Your Score: _____

Congratulations, Music Reader!

You've come so far, indeed!

Guide notes, intervals and ledger notes

you now can read.

So carry forth with practice,

and let your new skills grow,

Then play for friends and family

the music that you know.

_____

Your Name, Music Reader